T0353285

Kupferstich (1657) zu *L'histoire comique contenant les états et empires de la lune* von Cyrano de Bergerac

Glyn Maxwell

MASTERS ARE YOU MAD?

THE SEARCH FOR MALVOLIO

OBERON BOOKS
LONDON

WWW.OBERONBOOKS.COM

First published in 2012 by Oberon Books Ltd
521 Caledonian Road, London N7 9RH
Tel: +44 (0) 20 7607 3637 / Fax: +44 (0) 20 7607 3629
e-mail: info@oberonbooks.com
www.oberonbooks.com

A catalogue record for this book is available from the British Library.

PB ISBN: 978-1-84943-407-2
E ISBN: 978-1-84943-590-1

Cover design by Caroline Ogden on behalf of Chester Performs

Visit www.oberonbooks.com to read more about all our books and
to buy them. You will also find features, author interviews and news
of any author events, and you can sign up for e-newsletters so that
you're always first to hear about our new releases.

Dramatis Personae

THE CAPTAIN
an adventurer

OTTO
a ferryman

ORSINO
the Duke of Illyria

CORALINE
his boy, an actress

MARY BELCH
a disappointed wife

ADRIAN
an assassin

MIRALDA
a girl lost in the woods

JAGO
a traveller

SONGBIRD
a singer

MALVOLIO
formerly a steward

OLIVIA
formerly his mistress

A HARBOURMASTER

A MILLIONAIRE

A GENTLEMAN

A LADY

AN OLD MAN

The play takes place in Illyria and in the mountains
beyond, twelve years after the events depicted in
Twelfth Night.

Masters Are You Mad? The Search for Malvolio was first performed on July 13th 2012 in Grosvenor Park Open Air Theatre, Chester, in the third year of the summer season produced by Chester Performs. The play was staged in repertory with *Twelfth Night* by William Shakespeare.

Directed by Robin Norton-Hale
Designed by takis
Music composed by Harry Blake
Casting by Kay Magson

For Chester Performs:
Producer, Andrew Bentley
Artistic Director, Alex Clifton

The Captain, **Jonathan Glew**
Otto, **Chris Lindon**
Orsino, **Tom Radford**
Coraline, **Sarah Lambie**
Mary Belch, **Victoria Gee**
Adrian, **Haseeb Malik**
Miralda, **Krupa Pattani**
Jago, **Mark Rose**
Songbird, **Ellen O'Grady**
Malvolio, **Matthew Rixon**
Olivia, **Lorna Beckett**

Harbourmaster/Millionaire, **Chris Vincent**
Gentleman/Old Man, **Jack Lord**
Lady, **Scott Arthur**

ACT ONE

SCENE I

The harbour, Illyria. The CAPTAIN *in the crowd, showing a picture of a girl on a pendant, asking if anyone's seen her.* OTTO *comes, singing, carrying ropes*

OTTO	*None stronger than breath, no further from death,*
	One further from birth, each step on the earth
	My foot in my shoe, an itch on my foot,
	A bruise on my heel –
CAPTAIN	What kind of a song is that?
OTTO	It's a ferryman's song.
	Sing and it takes you away and it takes you back.
CAPTAIN	Doesn't any song do that?
OTTO	What do I care?
	It's a ferryman's song in that it's a ferryman singing.
	I carry ropes, as I have high hopes
	But I have no hopes, so I carry ropes
CAPTAIN	I can see you carry ropes! What country is this
	where they sing what's plain to see?
OTTO	Now there's a question.
	This is Illyria, matey.
CAPTAIN	Ah, I know it,
	it's on my chart.
OTTO	That warms us to the cockles,
	sir.
CAPTAIN	But I'm a hundred miles from there
	by my calculations.
OTTO	Give us an hour or two
	we'll pack our country up and set it down
	where your calculations say it is.
CAPTAIN	No need.
	I shall calculate again.
OTTO	If you wouldn't mind.
	Though, safe to say, it wouldn't take an hour

	to fold away what's left of us. This place
	is finished, matey. Cast your eye on these folks. *[audience]*
CAPTAIN	They came to greet my arrival here, so I find them
	hospitable at the least.
OTTO	They're all that's left.
	Daily they cluster here at the harbour wall,
	look longingly that way.
CAPTAIN	What do they look for?
OTTO	For the young, the beautiful, their departed darlings.
CAPTAIN	*Some* look young, *some* beautiful.
OTTO	You reckon?
	Then they'll be gone by nightfall. Their eyes
	are dreaming of a place their feet have never
	known.
CAPTAIN	What place is that?
OTTO	I don't know where,
	but all our youth are vanishing upriver.
	The golden boys and girls, the cream, the crop,
	the best and worst, the restless, the rest,
	all vanishing upriver. What they leave
	is a ship in the dust where once we had a township.
CAPTAIN	What's upriver?
OTTO	Mountains.
CAPTAIN	And what happens there?
OTTO	I've got no song about it.
CAPTAIN	So it isn't true if you've got no song about it?
OTTO	You're catching on.
CAPTAIN	Is imagination something
	foreign to you?
OTTO	Me I carry ropes.
CAPTAIN	Do you never dream of a better life?
OTTO	In my dreams
	the ropes pull *me*, there's that.
CAPTAIN	Well then I've come
	to a benighted land.
OTTO	*I* told *you* that.
CAPTAIN	I've seen so many realms. For one whole year
	I've roamed the world.

OTTO   One whole year? Ain't *you*
            the flying dutchman.

CAPTAIN   Yes, you probably wonder
            how have I kept my sanity. Here's how.   *[the pendant]*

OTTO   Is this your compass, sir? Or your little time-piece?
            Either way it's useless, it's a picture.

CAPTAIN   It's a picture of my girl.

OTTO   She's what you steer by?

CAPTAIN   In my heart, yes.

OTTO   (And he thinks my songs are stupid.)
            She's a pretty little island if the north
            is at the top.

CAPTAIN   Of course it's at the top.
            The north is always at the top.

OTTO *[turning it]*   Not now, look.
            The west is now and she's a whole new coastline.
            Good luck. My name is Otto.

CAPTAIN   What kind of a name is Otto?

OTTO   It's a ferryman's,
            the journey there and back are the same journey.
            Unlike the path she's taken.   *[the girl]*

CAPTAIN   What do you mean?

OTTO   She's heavenly, she's young. If you came this way
            in search of her there's little doubt she's gone
            where all Illyrians go.

CAPTAIN   Upriver...

OTTO   Upriver.

CAPTAIN   But she's not an Illyrian, she's like me,
            we're from the forest country, from Carinthia.

OTTO   Upriver doesn't care where people come from.
            The water lures them somehow, and they sail,
            sail up, swim up, battle through the jungle
            until the only water in this city
            trickles down the cheekbones of their mothers
            like your miracle on your little stone madonna.
            But what do I know...

CAPTAIN   Well if you know the water,
            and this life is ropes and dust and bruises, ferryman,
            why don't *you* sail upriver?

OTTO   I might do that
            sooner than I think and be paid, too.
            I am a man for hire.

CAPTAIN   Who's paying you
            to sail upriver?

OTTO   I...*am a man for hire.*

The CAPTAIN gets that OTTO wants to be paid to say more

OTTO   My wages come from even higher than you, sir.

CAPTAIN   Who rules here?

OTTO   The man who pays my wages.
            The Duke Orsino.

CAPTAIN   I'll play the duke. Go on.   *[pays more]*

OTTO   He needs a man escorted up as far
            as water carries anyone.

CAPTAIN   What man?

OTTO   The Blindman.

CAPTAIN   *The* blind man? What blind man?

OTTO   The one I'm meeting here.

CAPTAIN   What...do you *know*
            of the blind man?   *[pays more]*

OTTO   That he's due here.

CAPTAIN   I see.
            Do you know for a fact that he's blind?

OTTO   I never met him.

CAPTAIN   Might he not be undercover?

OTTO   Stranger things.

CAPTAIN   Why does the Duke Orsino want the blind man
            escorted up the river?

OTTO   I know nothing
            of the mission.

CAPTAIN   Good. Let's keep it that way.
            Just call me: The Blindman.

OTTO   I – missed my mark. I did not foresee The Blindman
            being a man of love, like you are.

CAPTAIN   Well,
            now you do.

OTTO   I'm to bring you to the palace,

boss, to take instructions for the journey.
From which, I pray to the god of ropes, we shall both
return.

CAPTAIN   I know we shall.

OTTO   How do you know?

CAPTAIN   Because I carry this. My Paloma.   *[pendant]*
Lead on.

OTTO   Mind if I sing?
Oh, he carries a locket in his breast pocket
He met some girl so he roams the world
No offence but he makes no sense

CAPTAIN   What was that?

OTTO   Nothing, boss.

CAPTAIN   Sing how I find Paloma, sing what's to be!

OTTO   Boss, I'd sooner go to sea in my slippers.

They go

SCENE II

CORALINE comes, holding a woman's wig

CORALINE   Let's get this straight: my name is Coraline.
I'm an actress, I'm a girl.
Try getting a job at the palace of this duke
with those credentials. Only boys work here,
but I got this far with bandages and banter,
so I start today. Let's see if I can remember:
I'm a girl called, what, 'Cesaria', and the duke
has no idea I'm a boy. I mean, in his story,
he has no idea I'm a boy. In real life
he has no idea I'm a girl, but work is work.

ORSINO *[from off]* Cesaria! Cesaria!

CORALINE puts the wig on as ORSINO comes

CORALINE   My lord?

ORSINO   The music, where's the music, I need music
as I come to you –

CORALINE	I am sorry my lord duke,
	your harpist has departed –
ORSINO	Not my harpist!
CORALINE	At dawn, I heard them say, they found the harpist's
	clothes all strewn about, no sign of him.
	He left his harp behind, its strings still blurred
	in sorrow by the window.
ORSINO	Upriver!
	Like the flautist and the fiddler, one by two
	by three I am abandoned! Not by you,
	Cesaria, you've stayed. Play what you play.
CORALINE	I – don't play anything. I – said I did,
	to get the job, there *are* no jobs in Illyria,
	my lord.
ORSINO	I think you're a girl.
CORALINE	That's right, to you
	I'm a girl.
ORSINO	Who I'm in love with.
CORALINE	No.
ORSINO	No?
CORALINE	My lord, not yet, we're playing the scene where you meet me.
	For the first time. To you I'm just the new, um,
	maid.
ORSINO	Precisely. Little do I know
	you're not a maid at all.
CORALINE	Or even a girl.
ORSINO	That's right. Or even a girl. I am in sweet, sweet
	ignorance of that. Say the words.
CORALINE	*I will strive to please you, lord.*
ORSINO	No, no! Turn away!
	Can you not remember a single thing I tell you,
	Cesaria? Your back is turned, when I enter
	you turn, you catch the light, *then* speak your words!
	Does no one care about my happiness?

They both notice MARY in the doorway

ORSINO	This person said she'd come. See what she wants.

ORSINO goes

MARY	That wig wouldn't fool an idiot.
CORALINE	What wig?

MARY is mortified – then CORALINE takes off the wig

CORALINE	The duke and I are rehearsing for a play.
MARY	I've been in plays like that. – *Cesaria…* *Cesario?* I know that name.
CORALINE	You do? So you know that all it takes to make a man is *O!* at the end, and to make a woman, *Ah…* This Duke appears to spend his hours surprised by vowels. Well, I'm the latest in a long line of Cesarias. I play Cesaria in this interlude we're doing then, suddenly, –
MARY	You cast off everything to reveal you're someone else, who you're also not.
CORALINE	You know, it's a job.
MARY	Did you ever meet the Duchess?
CORALINE	Duchess? There's a Duchess?
MARY	There was, ten years ago. They say she lost her taste for theatre, and sailed home where she came from. I suppose she got *un*-shipwrecked.
CORALINE	I don't know, it's my first day. My name is Coralin...us. What's yours, my lady?
MARY	I'm nobody's lady. I was a lady's maid then a man's habit. Sounds a bit like you.
CORALINE	I'm just an actor, ma'am. This has no meaning. All my friends are gone upriver.
MARY	Why d'you linger here?
CORALINE	Because, it's what...nobody else is doing.
MARY	So you stand out. On a desert you stand out.
CORALINE	On a first day I try my best. I'm required to ask you to state your business.
MARY	It was stated

in a letter that I wrote your duke. He knows
roughly why I'm here, it makes no difference
if he hears it from a maid who's not a maid
or an actress who's no actress.

CORALINE goes out. ORSINO comes

ORSINO   Lady Belch?

MARY   As ever till it's over.

ORSINO   How is your Lady Olivia's uncle?

MARY   I *have*
no lady, so no news on my lady's uncle,
my lord.

ORSINO   I am asking after your husband, woman.
Sir Toby, how's Sir Toby?

MARY   Ask that question
of creatures never seen by human eye.

ORSINO   What?

MARY   Of the Red Lion, ask that question,
or the Silver Monkey or the Four-Faced Dog
or the Green Man or the Elephant in his Castle
or any inn from *here* to wherever *there* is.
He's thirsty, and I'm hungry.
We always did divide the chores.

ORSINO   You say
you've something for me. What.

MARY   A thought.

ORSINO   What value's that?

MARY   As valuable
as the million-kroner notes you keep on printing.

ORSINO   We print money so that there'll *be more money*.
You know nothing of economics.

MARY   They make good hankies,
your million-kroner notes.

ORSINO   What was your thought...

MARY   It's about upriver.

ORSINO   Upriver? Fantasies.
Gold you can skim from water in your hands,
marble palaces where once were hovels,

millionaires where once were vagabonds,
angelic music, marriages in treetops,
all's light and sweet and what could this *be*
but nonsense, fictions, lies?

MARY   I heard a fable
of a forest camp where all the people smile,
where they wear these golden stockings, is the story,
ribboned with cross-garters, they say,
and the eyes you catch were hoping to catch yours,
for all who love are loved by those *they* love,
and it made me think of something.

ORSINO   I'm listening.

MARY   Because they also say there is a sage
who sees the future there, who tells fortunes
and every word comes true.

ORSINO   His name is Moai.

MARY   Moai...

ORSINO   That name was whispered down the grapevine
yesterday. We knew about this phantom
but now we have a name.

MARY   M-O-A-I?
Moai...Then my thought is a conviction.
That I might know this sage they say there is.
In my Lady Olivia's house he was the steward.
He's not been seen for years.

ORSINO   His name?

MARY   Malvolio.

ORSINO   Don't know him. Would you know him
if you saw him?

MARY   Yes, I would.

ORSINO   Would he know you?

MARY   Ye-es.

ORSINO   Would he trust you? Would he, Lady Belch?
...Whatever, it doesn't matter. You're going upriver.

MARY   I am?

ORSINO   Will your husband miss you? Didn't think so.
There's a room with a harp that way. Take what you need.
When you have helped to track down this man,

        this malcontent prophetic spouting butler,
        and all are home and all are reconciled
        and law-abiding here in my dukedom,
        I will personally relieve you, top to toe,
        of any debts you have, Mrs Lady Belch,
        and, if you wish it, any husband too.
        Why not have a think about –

MARY	Deal.
ORSINO	Good. Any other business?

MARY goes. CORALINE comes, with the CAPTAIN and OTTO

ORSINO	Which one of you's The Blindman?
OTTO	He is.

He took the form of a lovesick seafarer,
which is why I failed to –

ORSINO   Enough.
Some brilliant disguise, no doubt... Your
reputation goes before you, The Blindman.
Nightmare, nemesis! Did you not despatch
the warlike Red Rodolfo?

CAPTAIN   Who? Yes.

ORSINO   And the Archduke Franz Fitz Frederick, our foe?

CAPTAIN   Yes.

ORSINO   With arsenic, yes?

CAPTAIN   Might have been.

ORSINO   True, no need to know. Behold The Blindman...
He glides through towns and cities, he sees all,
he overhears, he undertakes. The *Blindman*...
Why are you called The Blindman, you're not blind.

CAPTAIN   Duke, because...my shadow goes before me,
so that people – wait – when they see me, I am always
walking from the west, with the sun behind me,
which blinds them, not me.

ORSINO   Yet the sun's not always
in the west.

CAPTAIN   No. At – dawn I arrive
from the east, so they're still blinded. Me, sun,
shadow and so forth.

OTTO	What if it's raining?
ORSINO	Shut up. We stand in awe.
	We hope to stand in debt. It is dark work
	I have hired you for. Have you discussed the mission?
CAPTAIN	No comment.
ORSINO	See? Truly professional.
	Cesaria, take the ferryman through there.
	You'll find a woman.
CORALINE	Um – ?
ORSINO	No an *actual* woman!
	The one who came before. She'll be going with you.
	Don't ask why, don't ask why not. Leave us.

CORALINE and OTTO go

ORSINO	Cesaria's her name. For all I know
	she's a girl.
CAPTAIN	Ri-ight.
ORSINO	No matter. Do you know him?
CAPTAIN	That boy? No.
ORSINO	She's not a boy!
CAPTAIN	I don't know him.
ORSINO	I mean: do you know the ferryman.
CAPTAIN	Not really.
	He met me at the harbour.
ORSINO	Do you know
	Mary Belch?
CAPTAIN	No comment.
ORSINO	They will help you
	find the man we want. We believe his name
	is Malvolio. When you've located him,
	act upon this. This is your Sealed Order.

ORSINO passes him a sealed letter

ORSINO	Open it only when you find the man.
	Act upon it at once. This, this – *Upriver*,
	this craze, this cult it's sucking all the lifeblood
	out of my dukedom. All the money's flowing
	outward like the city's been – upended.

Our young are being lied to, my friend,
infected by some radical foul creed
that eats away at – Oh,
but we miss these people so,
we do so want them safely home. I yearn
to speak with them, to hear their explanations,
I love their energy! But we need them back.
Poor old Illyria's thirsty. When you return
and the mission is accomplished, I will pay you
anything you want. What *do* you want?

CAPTAIN   Whatever we've – agreed.

ORSINO   We've not agreed
anything. A man who forgets details
is not a man to trust.

CAPTAIN   But a man who only
pretends to forget details...

ORSINO   Ah. The Blindman...
What's that around your neck?
Is that a pretty girl...

The CAPTAIN passes ORSINO his pendant

ORSINO   So you *are* a lovesick seafarer... And yet
you can do the work I've hired you for?

CAPTAIN   I can do
anything. What I do I do for her.

ORSINO   Bravo. You can have this girl. Take her, have her. *[pendant]*

CAPTAIN   She is mine already, my lord, but I can't find her.
The ferryman thinks she probably went upriver.

ORSINO   She probably did, and once we've solved the *problem*
of what's happening upriver, she'll be here,
in the happy family of Illyria... Deal?

CAPTAIN   Deal. Her name's Paloma.
She left our village suddenly last summer.
In the note she left she said she'd change the world.
When we were children, oh, we dreamed we'd do that.
But I thought –

ORSINO   Aah, you thought you'd do it *together*,
didn't you... *I* want the world to change
myself, did I mention that? That's why I love

these dreamers in the mountains, I was once
a thing of that – ilk. Oh we'll find your honey,
then together *you change anything you choose to.*
First, find Moai. Enter, Cesaria.

CORALINE brings OTTO and MARY

ORSINO	The Blindman, this is Mary Belch. She knows
	the man by sight and he knows her. She'll help you
	find him. Understand? You work for me now.
	Boatman, is your boat where we agreed?
OTTO	Just back there, at the inlet by the trees. *[the Dee]*
ORSINO	No one'll see you there. Cesaria, take them.
	Then come straight back to me. Well not *straight* back
	but do come back in time. But soon, to me.

CORALINE leads the CAPTAIN, OTTO and MARY away

ORSINO   Music. Music…music, music ho!…
           IS THERE ANYBODY LEFT???

Someone starts feebly playing a triangle. ORSINO roars in exasperation

SCENE III

*The Harbour. The real Blindman, ADRIAN, has arrived. He dresses all in black
and wears the world's first pair of sunglasses. The HARBOURMASTER comes with a
customs form*

HARBOUR	Name, please. Name, please, sir. What is your name?
	You can't just pitch up here without a name, sir,
	we may've seen better times but we do have standards.
ADRIAN	I am silent for good reason.
HARBOUR	You can put your
	reasons for silence there, in Box B5.
ADRIAN	I am on government business.
HARBOUR	Ditto, sunshine.
	I need a name. Scrawl it if you have to.

ADRIAN sighs, takes the form, writes, and gives the form back

HARBOUR *[loudly]* 'ADRIAN *AGUECHEEK*?' Is that your name?

ADRIAN   It's not the name I go by!

HARBOUR	Like I care.
ADRIAN	I have cold and silent motives of my own
	to write no more.
HARBOUR	'Reason for visit' there,
	that one's an obligation.
ADRIAN	Reason for visit?
HARBOUR	'Profession', that one too, if you wouldn't mind.

ADRIAN irritably writes, and gives the document back

HARBOUR	'SECRET MISSION'? 'HIRED ASSASSIN'? Blimey,
	I can see why you was reluctant.
ADRIAN	Look shut up!
	Do you think you know my story now?
HARBOUR	Beg pardon?
ADRIAN	I am a man of silence. I say nothing.
	Do you think my name can tell you anything?
HARBOUR	It tells me you're an Aguecheek –
ADRIAN	It's a lie!
	I am no more an Aguecheek than you, sir!
	I left them floundering long ago, that pair
	who pleased themselves to pluck me from the slums,
	yet lavished all on my limp-wit elder brother,
	the cash, the mansion, and the music lessons –
	I could play the viol-de-gamboys if my parents
	bought me a viol-de-gamboys, but no,
	they got me a cup and ball and shut the door,
	and I heard their voices chuckle away like water.
	They should have called me *Fido* Aguecheek!
HARBOUR	Why's that then, sir.
ADRIAN	Shut up!
	I am a man of brooding silence.
HARBOUR	Right then.
	Good day, sir.

ADRIAN grabs the form back

ADRIAN	*Secret mission? Hired assassin?*
	It doesn't tell you *why*, it's the effect
	and not the cause, you want to know the cause?

HARBOUR   Well I ought to get this processed –

ADRIAN   I was nine,
                 there were frolics on the lawn, my brother's friends
                 were tossing him in the muddy pool as normal,
                 and I heard him shout *hooray!* and *tally-ho!*
                 as if he liked it, so they turned on me,
                 I, weak, bespectacled (a future half-blue
                 at spelling had they only thought to ask me
                 some difficult long words) but oh no,
                 oh no, it was that muddy pool for me,
                 that hellhole, that malebolge, I was soon
                 embedded in the earth and when I rose
                 from the Adrian-shaped pit I had been plunged in,
                 my glasses were begoggled with the filth.
                 They shrieked, those boys, they played at blind man's bluff,
                 and, deep in the encrustment of my suffering,
                 besplattered by the bestial tide of vile
                 humanity, did I become...The Blindman.
                 Cold I became, and silent, and brooding.
                 That day, that long-forgotten Saturday
                 the eighth of June, at five fifteen, I changed.
                 I altered. I evolved from earth. I became
                 this man of cold dark silence. Hm.
                 And yet you still stand there. I've nothing for you.
                 Nothing for any man.

HARBOUR   I need the copy,
                 the pink one. Keep the yellow one for your files.

ADRIAN screws up the form. The HARBOURMASTER menaces him

ADRIAN   Files? I defy files!

HARBOUR   Mr Aguecheek,
                 you've done it now, you –

ADRIAN   It's not Aguecheek it's *Blindman!*

Daggers are drawn. CORALINE comes, flashing a warrant

CORALINE   Hold in the name of the Duke! You're The Blindman?

ADRIAN   Normally I would keep my cool counsel,
                 and no one guess what way my eyes are looking
                 or on what fearful plane my mind is working
                 but I shall break my silence to affirm
                 that I am indeed...The Blindman.

CORALINE   Harbourmaster,
                I am Orsino's man, I'll deal with this.

The HARBOURMASTER *goes*

CORALINE   (I *say* I'll deal with this. But what to do?
                The wrong man's in the river-boat. Orsino
                will strangle the first throat that utters this!
                I believe I'm going to quit on my first day.)

ADRIAN   Are you the ferryman who was meant to meet me?

CORALINE   No, I'm – a passer-by.

ADRIAN   I heard you say
                distinctly you're Orsino's man.

CORALINE   We all are,
                no? Except when some of us are women.

ORSINO *heard approaching*

ORSINO   Cesaria! Where's my Cesaria?
                I don't mean *my* Cesaria, I mean
                my *maid* Cesaria, she's just a girl –

CORALINE *runs away and hides as* ORSINO *arrives*

ORSINO   You! What is your name?

ADRIAN   I say nothing.
                I am silent as the oak.

ORSINO   My name's Orsino.
                I cut down oaks for coffee tables.

ADRIAN   Adrian
                Aguecheek at your service, also known
                as The Blindman.

ORSINO   *What? WHAT?*

ADRIAN   I was hired, your grace, to track and terminate
                the man responsible for the disorders
                upriver. I was due here when I duly
                arrived.

ORSINO   That treacherous captain and his fool
                ferryman, they've gone!

ADRIAN   I need no ferry,
                lord, I'll move on foot through the high forest,
                following the river's line, concealed

> by darkness, brooding silence and the skills
> of an experienced desperado.

ORSINO　　Find them.
> There are three of them in the boat, two men and a woman.
> The woman will lead you to him. When you find him,
> the heart of this resistance, this poison,
> this infernal steward Moai,
> you do for him, and do for them: the woman,
> the impostor *and* the boatman, understand?
> Yours is the only face I want to see
> returning from Upriver. Take this.　　　　*[a banknote]*
> It's a billion-kroner note.

ADRIAN　　I am The Blindman.
> I am worth more.

ORSINO scribbles on the note

ORSINO　　It's a trillion now.

ADRIAN　　　　Thank you.

ADRIAN takes the money and runs away into the trees

ORSINO　　Cesaria! Cesaria!

ORSINO goes. ADRIAN, having run the wrong way, runs on and off again. CORALINE emerges

CORALINE　　Do for him and do for them? I thought this
> some kind of rescue, but he's planning murder!
> Of everyone he sent there. And that fool's　　*[Adrian]*
> fanatical enough to get the job done.
> Had I run thirty yards away, not twenty,
> I'd not have heard a thing, I'd have quit my job
> and stretched out like the world of a Saturday.
> But now the mountain calls. I can't stand by.
> To stop that man I'd better stay a man,
> run like a man – make a plan – run while I plan!
> Outfool this fool somehow. And what's my wage?
> Some kind of happy ending? Turn that page!

CORALINE runs off after ADRIAN

ACT TWO

SCENE I

Some way upriver. The CAPTAIN *and* MARY *are sitting round a fire.* OTTO *sings off into the distance. Far away a similar song comes back*

OTTO   *Ten by day and nine by night*
                       Cross at by-way weeds at right
                       Watch for point at seven turn
                       Left impassable October

CAPTAIN   I mean, what is it, modern poetry?
                       It makes no sense at all, it pretends to beauty,
                       'night' and 'right' I like, I know where I stand
                       with 'night and 'right', I feel I'm being sung to,
                       but what's a 'seven turn' and on what sea
                       is that a rhyme for 'passable October'?
                       It's not even October!

MARY   He told you,
                       Blindman, he is singing what he hears
                       from higher up the hillside. Obviously
                       he should have rhymed the thing so you'd remember,
                       so instead of navigating like his job is
                       he should be twanging tunes for our campfire pleasure.

CAPTAIN   Well he should be. He can navigate by day.
                       The night-time on a journey is the time
                       for stories, and memories by firelight.

MARY   Memories? Precious little to remember
                       here, were you not looking at the river?
                       A stream at noon, a trickle by teatime,
                       and now a patchwork of these starlit puddles.
                       This journey's over.

CAPTAIN   This – this *is* upriver?

    OTTO *comes by*

OTTO   What they're singing is: the river's dammed,
                       a mile further up, clogged with something,

	so the streams are running ways they never ran
	and switching fast as even they can sing it.
CAPTAIN	Wait wait who's *they*?
MARY	I told you.
OTTO	My kindred,
	all the boatmen, the brothers of the mudbanks,
	they sing what they can see.
CAPTAIN	Yes, like him
	they don't *do* beauty, do you,
	they don't *do* things like, oh, imagination.
OTTO	No boss, they're not the songs to stop the world,
	I grant you, they say things like 'row to starboard',
	'mind the bank', they sprinkle the odd joke in,
	but these days not so much. Well, to my post...

OTTO goes back to the edge of the trees, and listens to the distant river-song

CAPTAIN	Why don't they use a map?
MARY	Yes, good idea.
	Or something useful, like your pendant there.
CAPTAIN	Lady, one man's hat is another's cap.
MARY	Roams the world a year – behold his wisdom!
	What will the ages bring, perhaps 'the moon
	is not the sun' or 'little things get bigger'.
CAPTAIN	Her name is Paloma. We two grew up together.
MARY	I quite forgot I even asked her name
	but I must have done as here's you telling me.
CAPTAIN	In the valley was our time, and the woods of elm
	we ran through, we would sing to one another.
MARY	You could have got a job up here.
CAPTAIN	*Love*-songs,
	not 'turn left at the weedbank'. One blue evening
	we vowed to change the world, to make it better,
	and every May renewed those vows. Last summer –
	oh it feels like yesterday – we had a quarrel,
	we fought, we slept unreconciled and I,
	in rosy light of dawn grown mad –
MARY	Though not
	too mad for poetry, clearly.

CAPTAIN	– Did light out
	for the grey heavens. I left to change the world,
	and four whole seasons, isolate in sorrow,
	are my reward.
MARY	Poor isolate poor you.
	Why didn't you turn round?
CAPTAIN	I did turn round.
	I strode to the next valley, spent three nights
	in bitter contemplation and regret,
	at drinking and shove-ha'penny with strangers,
	then I returned.
MARY	And she was gone.
CAPTAIN	That day.
	Her letter said *she'd* gone to change the world.
	Four whole seasons have I searched for her.

OTTO, listening to the trees, can hear the faint sound of a girl crying

OTTO	Do you hear that? Does anyone hear that?
CAPTAIN	Friend ferryman, we are busy at our sacred
	firelight reminiscence... Four whole seasons
	I searched for her.
MARY	Correct me if you care to,
	but I think your tale took longer than four seasons.
CAPTAIN	The world is wide.
MARY	Ooh, let me write that down.
CAPTAIN	In what she'd left of summer when she'd gone
	I sought her in the dales and meadows, ranging
	wider, further outwards. In the autumn
	I stalked the friendless cities, asking questions,
	watching windows, watching windows darken
	as a shadow blew a candle. By the new year
	I was in the wilderness, in a winter wasteland.
	I sought the Hermit...
MARY	Any old hermit, is that?
CAPTAIN	He lives at the edge of all known maps.
MARY	Except
	his own, I guess, where he's slap-bang in the middle.
CAPTAIN	He told me life was a journey.

MARY	Any other revelations?
CAPTAIN	That winter turns to spring.
MARY	Wonder of winter wonders. And who pays for this odyssey of yours?
CAPTAIN	I pay, my friend, oh, I pay.
MARY	That's not quite what I meant.
CAPTAIN	Have you never loved, my friend? Never sat in an empty world?
MARY	Does a kitchen count? (No, to the other question.)
CAPTAIN	As spring came –
MARY	As the wise man said it would –
CAPTAIN	I joined a Bohemian fishing boat, we plied our trade along this coast.
MARY	Does Bohemia *have* boats? It's got no coast.
CAPTAIN	Well I mentioned that and they made me Captain. Slowly, one by one, the boys abandoned ship and I ran aground. And now I know they probably journeyed here.
MARY	Right... And you've done all that since last summer? Time's elastic stuff for you, eh Blindman and no mistake. It's taken me twelve years of wedlock to make one enormous scarf, now he says he can't stand the colours. What's that sound?
CAPTAIN	Another lullaby from the mudbank brothers.
MARY	Not them, from the other way.

From the other direction, they hear a distant, beautiful song

SONG	*What you would be* *Will be* *Aye* *By and by* *All you would be will be* *Only you and only* *What you would be...*
MARY	A woman is singing, higher up the mountain.

CAPTAIN	The voice of Moai?
MARY	Moai is a man, though...
	It's – heavenly.
CAPTAIN	Paloma sang that way.
MARY	Of course she did.
CAPTAIN	She said she'd change the world
	some day.
MARY	Hush.
CAPTAIN	I said I'd change it somehow.
MARY	Hush.
CAPTAIN	Why did they send you on this journey?
	That's how we roll by firelight: one story
	then another, no one judges.
MARY	No one judges?
	I judged yours. I judged it to be horseshit.
	So judge mine, feel free. I took a man
	I didn't like and broke him into pieces
	as if he would have broken me.
CAPTAIN	And would he?
MARY	(The song's gone.) Would he have broken me?
	No. He would have bothered me to doomsday
	but not beyond. I'm here because I know him,
	I can help, I can identify the bits.
	We can row him home in boxes. Go on, judge me.
CAPTAIN	If it's true, you did him wrong.
MARY	So you despise me
	and suspect I'm lying, don't you love
	the campfire. What's that sound? Where's Otto?
OTTO	Asleep, awake, alive.
CAPTAIN	We heard singing.
	Not boatman-fare, a faraway sweet music.
OTTO	Ignore it.
CAPTAIN	Easier said.
OTTO	It was without
	instructions.
CAPTAIN	Oh so ignore the moon.
OTTO	No, boss,

the moon says go to sleep.

MARY   I didn't mean
the singing, I heard someone in the bushes.

OTTO   Show yourself, who goes there?

A rustle in the bushes and the 'MILLIONAIRE' emerges, filthy, dazed

OTTO   An unarmed man, no danger.
We have a fire, we've food –

CAPTAIN   Is that the man
you know?

MARY   Of course it's not.

CAPTAIN   Tell me, friend,
are you the Voice of Moai?

MARY   Oh very subtle, Blindman.

MILLIONAIRE   Moai... Moai...

CAPTAIN   Thank you. Sir, what do you know of Moai?

MILLIONAIRE Gate...the gate...

CAPTAIN   Gate, what about a gate?
Answer me!

OTTO   Hey easy.

MARY   He's frightened.
Let him have some – listen. Listen.

The Song again, far off. The 'MILLIONAIRE' suddenly straightens, rapt

MILLIONAIRE They'll come here by and by.

CAPTAIN   What did you say?

MILLIONAIRE The carriages are due. From far and wide
they're on the move.

CAPTAIN   What carriages, what gate?

MILLIONAIRE For the Grand Reunion Ball in my Summer Palace!
My suit is pressed.

CAPTAIN   Do you – know where you are, my friend?

MILLIONAIRE I am escorting Mademoiselle Claudette
along the cloisters, down the colonnade,
arm in silken arm, she winks, she loves me,
and in the courtyard at the open gateway
everyone we ever knew is beckoning
come join us here without delay! I barely
know which – eyes to meet –

The Siren-Song fades and he stoops, in ruins, the vision gone

CAPTAIN	Sir? Monsieur?
OTTO	He's dreaming where he stands.
MARY	Somebody fooled *him* line and sinker.

The 'MILLIONAIRE' suddenly staggers away into the trees

CAPTAIN	Monsieur!
MARY	Oh let him be.
OTTO	If you think a song's for you, at the song's end you think yourself abandoned.
CAPTAIN	A gate, he said a gate.
OTTO	He did, he also said he had a summer palace. Life and language split into two streams. Like these new streams here there and everywhere. From this point upward it can't be navigated. We're walking.
CAPTAIN	I don't like this.
MARY	You're The Blindman, you signed up.
CAPTAIN	Well, no and yes.
OTTO	Companions, pack your stuff. The river can't help us now. I'll listen out for signals from my kin, but all they're saying is: nothing makes no sense where we're heading. No geography, no history, no language.
MARY	And here's where all the young Illyrians came.
CAPTAIN	Here's where Paloma is, and I *will* find her.
OTTO	Let's find this Moai first, boss, then we all go home rewarded. Off we go.
CAPTAIN	Lead on.

OTTO leads MARY and the CAPTAIN on through the trees

SCENE II

ADRIAN runs on, looks lost, finds someone in the audience

ADRIAN You are probably afraid. You don't know where
my eyes are roaming or my mind is racing.
I'm a man of silence. I now break that silence
only because those Path-finding lessons
on the Silver Duke-of-Salzburg Award
were wasted on my brother, who'd be hard-pressed
to find the clam in a clam-shell! Oh, my work
was always city work, the streets and alleys,
in dark straight lines I'd wend my silent way.
Out here I try to brood for just a moment
when something bites me or I bang my head.

So I seem to be slightly, momentarily lost,
stranger: did you see two men go by,
and a woman and, if so, in which direction?
Thank you. (If you know what's good for you
this never happened.) *En garde!*

ADRIAN hears the approach of CORALINE and swiftly has a knife to her throat

ADRIAN Passer-by, you cannot pass by me.
I am blind in name alone.

CORALINE I'm glad I found you,
Blindman. I was looking for you.

ADRIAN You were?
Why?

CORALINE I know you're doing the Duke's good work,
and I wondered if I could help.

ADRIAN Oh. Can you run?

CORALINE Not as fast as you.

ADRIAN Can you find paths?

CORALINE No better than the next.

ADRIAN Can you lie low?

CORALINE Evidently not.

ADRIAN Can you destroy?

CORALINE Frankly no.

ADRIAN Those are what I live by.
In what manner can you help me?

CORALINE	I can – talk.
ADRIAN	Why so can I, except I am by instinct
	silent at all times, except, of course,
	then, when I was talking, and, and, now.
	Not now, but then. I mean, not then, but, well.
CORALINE	It seems to me you need a man to talk,
	to ask for this and answer that and generally
	free you up for your dark brooding labours.
ADRIAN	Are you saying I need a fool?
	Do I *look* like I need a fool?
CORALINE	No, not at all.
	But a fool is what I am, I would be honoured
	to be your fool.
ADRIAN	You mean, to jumble language
	pointlessly and stir the words like soup
	when nothing much is happening?
CORALINE	Precisely.
	People will think us harmless.
ADRIAN	You *are* harmless.
	I'm not.
CORALINE	Indeed sir, prithee,
	what is a harmless juggler?
ADRIAN	I don't know, fool.
CORALINE	Why, no juggler at all, not having harms.
	Arms. Not having arms.

ADRIAN stares in utter silence. Then he absolutely wees himself with laughter, as if he hasn't laughed since childhood. Then suddenly stops and is cool again

ADRIAN	Fool, that was magnificent. Attend me.

ADRIAN runs off, with CORALINE after him

SCENE III

Silence. The woods. A 'GENTLEMAN' comes, in rags, pawing at the earth

GENTLEMAN   Moai...Moai...Moai...

Suddenly a 'LADY' runs in, likewise derelict and mad, she attacks him, they fight, scratching and biting, until the Siren-Song begins again. Then they stand up straight, lovers long ago. They waltz together, gazing into each other's eyes

GENTLEMAN	I knew it was you.
LADY	I knew it was you first.
GENTLEMAN	I knew at the Castle.
LADY	I knew at the steeplechasing.
GENTLEMAN	You're wearing what you wore then...
LADY	You're dancing like you danced then!
GENTLEMAN	It was sunny/cloudy/raining then... *[whatever the weather is]*
LADY	It's sunny/cloudy/raining now for us...
GENTLEMAN	We walked the Roman walls.
LADY	We walked them twice, a ring for you and a ring for me my darling..
BOTH	Then through the Gate we go...

They imagine they are dancing in Grosvenor Park, where they first kissed. OTTO, MARY and the CAPTAIN have crept in and are watching them dance. The waltz ends, the Siren-Song fades. The lovers crumble away from each other, stare with mutual hatred and flee in different directions

CAPTAIN	So rapidly it comes and goes, true love...
MARY	Did your hermit tell you that?
OTTO	It's that music, they seem in thrall to it like the wealthy gent in rags.
MARY	True love, but like in silly plays it comes and goes.
CAPTAIN	You heard them, they're in love, they walked the walls! You're all cynics, you Illyrians, you take a leaf from *my* book.
MARY	Your book is a leaflet, chum, we have volumes.
OTTO	Pay no heed to this song, I would beg you, ma'am, Blindman.
CAPTAIN	*Will do,* ferryman without a ferry, boatman on foot, give us the song about how you've got toothache, or how your shirt was *not* torn and now *is* torn, or how your river-knowledge guided us

somewhere there's no knowledge and no river,
oh capture the moment, do!

OTTO You're quite right.
Out of the stream what earthly use am I?

CAPTAIN *He* said it, not me.

MARY You're one of us,
our friend, we've come this far.

OTTO I don't believe
we ought to go no further.

CAPTAIN Is he mad?

OTTO You'll find no gold upriver, no dream,
no palace and no true-love, all's mirage,
illusion.

Again OTTO thinks he hears a girl crying

OTTO But – illusion with a rope
that pulls, can no one else hear that?

MARY Hear what?
I heard a song I hope to hear again,
but nothing more.

CAPTAIN You're contracted, we all are.
Once we've found this Moai,
once we've brought him back like the duke said,
your fee is paid, her debts are cleared, and I,
I marry my Paloma. Duke Orsino
said he'd deploy the whole of his police force
to trace her!

OTTO Boss, you ought to have been a priest.

CAPTAIN Why?

OTTO You do so like believing things.

MARY We will find the man we're seeking.
I feel it in my soul. I do have one,
ferryman, though I keep it in my cellar
with the fruit for making jam. We'll find Malvolio
because I've something for him, look…here…   *[letter]*
One day at the harbour my lady passed by me,
asked me if I remembered her, 'My lady!
Of course!' said I, but she said 'I'm no one's lady.'
She told me: 'Bear this letter to the man

> whose name it bears,' I read – *Malvolio* –
> looked up, and she was gone. It's yellow now,
> the name's discoloured. But I will find this man
> and all that was done shall be undone.

OTTO   My friends,
> you're not the souls you were at sea level.
> All people seem like dreamers to *my* mind,
> but you two are taking flight. If you *will* go further,
> then with you I will go,
> I am your guide, though I'm as good a guide now
> as fireflies to a sailor in his drink.
> Still, my nose says this way, both barrels.

OTTO leads on. MARY and the CAPTAIN follow

SCENE IV

ADRIAN runs on, with CORALINE, panting and exhausted, in his wake. ADRIAN goes to the same person in the audience

ADRIAN   You are probably terrified. I understand that.
> My fool would fright you further were he not
> so scant of breath. I break my accustomed silence
> to say to you I think I know your sister.
> I met her back that way. She was good enough
> to point me where she saw a group of three,
> two male, one female, enemies of freedom,
> progressing up the mountain. I am a gifted
> tracker, I seek only confirmation.
> This way? That way? That way?
> Thank you. Fool, befuddle this bystander,
> so that she quite forgets us.

CORALINE   Can't – can't speak –

ADRIAN   The one about the juggler, if you please!

CORALINE   I can't – just wait –

ADRIAN   I can't, it's just too perfect.
> What do you call a juggler without arms?
> Ha! You don't know? An armless juggler! There!
> That's funny, isn't it! Ha!

CORALINE   That – isn't – how it goes –

ADRIAN   Hm, curious...
                  It's turned unfunny. In fact it's turning sad.
                  Which shows – I could have been a *tragic* player
                  as well as a comedian, but that free term
                  at the Royal Academy of Delightful Arts
                  in London, who do you think got that? *Mais oui!*
                  My witless *frère*, that overrated sot
                  who thought a soliloquy a type of pudding!
                  While that same year, well hidden from the ages,
                  I placed fourth in the egg-and-spoon at school.
                  A personal best but who remembers that?
                  Osvaldo's spoon was larger. I said nothing.
                  Or nothing until now. Attend me, fool.

ADRIAN runs off, CORALINE glances back, thinks she sees something

CORALINE   I thought I saw a – oh but this exertion
                  is thinning all my senses to their limits.
                  I have to stop this idiot somehow!

CORALINE staggers off. ORSINO comes, as a Lady-in-mourning

ORSINO   Only by speaking out in this lonely glade
                  can I address the strangeness of the juncture
                  I find myself arrived at. In my dress –
                  I mean, in my *ad*dress – to the loyal foliage,
                  I speak as man and yet I feel as woman.
                  I must, for safety, to convince as woman,
                  for who on Illyrian soil would harm a woman?
                  – (Let's not dwell there, I mean who'd harm a woman
                  vulgarly, when I do harm I do it
                  for the state, for principle, morality,
                  for example ordering, say, some termination
                  for the good of the body politic and so on) –
                  Oh I'm no debater, am I, I'm a woman!
                  I've a lot going on in my head, you know, just now!
                  I go as woman, yet – I am *as man.*
                  As man my mind is intricate but clear.
                  He is missing. My Cesario. Cesario,
                  my employee. I missed him,
                  in that I noted that: he was not there.
                  Clarity of a male. I did not care

that he was not. As woman – and as stated,
I go as woman merely for my safety –
(I would scarcely go for comfort, all these things
that clasp and cradle me where I've no need
of cradling quite so tightly – that said,
I am kept warm, my man's cold mind concedes,
I am kept quite reminded of my confines
in a peculiar, not unpleasing,) – Where was I?
He is missing. All the nine Cesarios
preceding him went missing, yet not once
did I stir from my bed. O my Cesario!
(That was my woman's mind. When I don't need that,
I shall cast it off forever, like this dress.
Though I may conserve this dress, its encasing silk
will one day please some person, some lady.)
I don't know where I am. Nobody heard me.

ORSINO lowers his veil and hurries on

ADRIAN runs on, and goes to the same person in the audience

ADRIAN　　　Fear has frozen you. And yet *I* know *you*.
Your cousins further down were most helpful
in pointing me the way I knew already.
Item one: two males,
one female, that way? this way? or that?
Item two: a figure veiled in black,
possibly on our tail, sex uncertain,
this way? that way? this?

CORALINE stumbles in, exhausted

CORALINE　　　It's the same – person –

ADRIAN　　　Who is the same, the figure veiled in black?

CORALINE　　　You keep asking – the same person – for directions –

ADRIAN　　　Don't mind him, he's my fool. Do some fooling.

CORALINE drops to the ground exhausted. ADRIAN stares, then doubles up

ADRIAN　　　Top-class tomfoolery! He was standing up!
Then he fell right down, look at that!

CORALINE　　　Oh good grief...

ADRIAN stops laughing abruptly, and looks at the helpful audience-member

ADRIAN   Remember the name: The Blindman. Tell your cousins.
                Forget you ever met me.
                Remember – not to remember.
                There is – no contradiction.

He begins to realise there is, and runs off. CORALINE rises

CORALINE   My name is Coraline and what of that?
                I have no place or post, and all my girlfriends
                left for the highlands long ago. I left
                my job on my first day. I merit nothing.

The Siren-song begins. CORALINE, transported, sees an audience before her

CORALINE   And yet, and yet, at lonely times like these
                how I seem to be hearing music... Then I see
                oh all around me like a rainbow – ladies,
                lords and children, smiling almost sadly,
                or, if not smiling, watching me intently
                with an ancient generosity. Then I feel
                there is no situation I could fall in
                that I could not, in some way, by sometimes speaking
                truly to these lovely apparitions,
                resolve or solve or sweeten, that the days
                are pages turning to that happy ending...

The song fades

CORALINE   And then it fades and sure the world's no story,
                and no one knows my name. I was just a fool
                when I was young for all I *was* was young.
                Oh I had the heart to help, but not the lungs.

CORALINE runs after ADRIAN

SCENE V

OTTO, MARY and the CAPTAIN soldier on, lost

OTTO   *Slopes to left*
                Stump by boulder
                Branches crossing
                Work of humans
                Air gone thinner

Moth mosquito
Air gone colder

CAPTAIN Please make him stop. I heard an angel singing
and when her song was over, and all sound
had knelt in awe of melody, up piped
this inland mariner with his to-do list.

OTTO If we know the way we came, when we turn round
we turn my words and thus we know the way
we can get back –

CAPTAIN I get the principle!
It's just the ugliness, the –

MARY Hush, she's singing...

The Song starts up again far away. MARY and the CAPTAIN transfixed again

CAPTAIN She's singing to me of June it was, late June,
with evenings light as if God held his breath,
and we played our tracking games in the little wood
we could see our houses from, she'd set these arrows
from twigs I'd stumble on, I always found her!
Or she found me.

MARY She's singing of November,
November in our lives, when all our sins
sit heavy on us and we bow our heads
for all the saints to pass – only, look up,
she sings, a lamp in the woods ahead, the glow
of Christmastime when all the lost come homeward,
the man to his household, overseeing all,
as the coloured lanterns glint in his carving knife,
the diligent high steward...

OTTO *Stony ground now*
Forest dense
View of summit
Falcons circling

*The CAPTAIN and MARY move on, entranced. OTTO follows then stops. The Song
continues ahead, but behind him again he can hear crying. He retraces his steps*

OTTO *Falcons circling*
View of summit

> *Forest dense*
> *Stony ground...*

MIRALDA comes, dishevelled, holding a rag as if it was her baby

OTTO	What's the matter, friend?
MIRALDA	I am so sleepy.
OTTO	Why are you tired, friend?
MIRALDA	It never stops,
	she cries and cries.
OTTO	But, friend, it is you who's crying.
MIRALDA	No. I'm happy. Look. See. I'm smiling.
	I love my little Lula.
OTTO	Can I – hold her?

MIRALDA passes the rag to OTTO

OTTO	Does Lula like the song of the woods?
MIRALDA	She loves it,
	she's just like me, I love it.
OTTO	So. Perhaps
	she'll be a singer one day, little Lula.

OTTO passes the 'baby' back. The Song stops. MIRALDA drops the rag as if it were nothing. OTTO automatically goes to 'save' it, picks it up and returns it to MIRALDA, who drops it again and stands there as if catatonic

OTTO   So. A rag is a rag. (You knew that, Otto.)
          I've – seen your face before. Not as a face, though,
          as a picture on a pendant, and the pendant
          is round the neck of a captain, do you know him,
          he goes by the name of Blindman, but he sees,
          he sees you, and, and yet, you seem no older
          than a *daughter* would have got by now. But you –
          are his, it seems. Paloma. His Paloma.
          I wish – that were not as it is, but I admit
          I'm not your man for *what if,* or *if only.*

He gives her his coat

OTTO   I'm a man for the proper coat in the proper weather.
          Will you come with me, I'll bring you to your – master?
          Lover? What? No sign of him on you.
          Where are your mother and father?

MIRALDA drops to the ground and weeps. OTTO sits by her, puts his arm round her, takes out a scrap of bread for her. She eats, her eyes closed

OTTO   Hey hey,
                no need to say. I had them too, you know.
                Not as in mummy-and-daddy, I never had that,
                except when I was smaller than a memory.
                No, as in father's house and mother's cottage,
                on either side of a lake. My father pushed me
                out on a boat, my ears boxed and burning
                with his fury at my mother, facts to tell her,
                and other times she'd do the same, my cheeks
                scarlet with appeals to make to him,
                and yet, out there on the water, in the middle,
                his anger and her desolation seemed
                to meet somehow and mingle in the gentle
                ripples that were all my boat could make.
                I belonged to both of them as I tied the ropes
                on the jetty by my father's house, on the bank
                by my mother's. They were trying to recruit a soldier
                but they made a ferryboat-man.

MIRALDA stands up and points up the mountain

OTTO   What lies that way? That song.
                That's where your master's gone to. I'm his guide.
                But I lost him, like you did, and he lost you.
                Let's find him, eh? But first, let's find you
                and let's find me. I'll look where your eyes are looking,
                sail by them stars. Call it the long way home.
                Here, for when your song starts.

OTTO offers, then pockets, the rag, and they go where MIRALDA is pointing

SCENE VI

ORSINO comes, as a Lady-in-mourning, and is jumped by ADRIAN

ADRIAN   Foul stalker, end of story!
ORSINO   I am a woman!
                If I were a man I'd fight, but I am a woman

	so I throw myself on your manly mercy!
ADRIAN	The Blindman
	casts no shadow but you've dogged my way
	from the river to this wilderness. Why?
ORSINO	I seek the man called Moai, I am a woman
	and I hear he can make my dreams come true!
ADRIAN	I hear
	he'll die before he does. How have you tracked me
	all this way? I can outrun the greyhound.
	Well the beagle, anyway, nearly. I can outrun
	the wild sheep, and this girl and her many cousins *[same person]*
	have guided me five miles into the highlands,
	so how have you kept up with me?
ORSINO	I don't know!
	I can't read maps and I don't know what to do next,
	I'm changeable and helpless in your power!

CORALINE catches up, panting

CORALINE	Blindman, what are you doing?
ADRIAN	She is a witness,
	she saw everything, she must die.
ORSINO	Oh spare me!
	I didn't see anything, I was too flustered!
CORALINE	Blindman, you haven't *done* anything yet,
	there's nothing to have witnessed!
ADRIAN	A wise point, and yet it's a fool who makes it.
	Wisdom in folly, eh... I expect they teach that
	at the Austrian School of Paradox, then again,
	how the hell would I know?

ADRIAN lets ORSINO go

CORALINE	You need to leave a trail of the terrified,
	Blindman, then your fame will be spread further.
ADRIAN	I will keep her as a hostage.
CORALINE	Er, why?
ADRIAN	For bargaining.
CORALINE	But The Blindman doesn't bargain.
ADRIAN	No. He does not. – I want her for a hostage!
ORSINO	You mean, I'll be made to travel with you both,

	at a forced pace, in my widow's weeds?
ADRIAN	You shall!
ORSINO	Then I embrace my dismal fate.
CORALINE	Good grief...
ADRIAN	Fool and hostage, silence!
	I am a man of silence and I sow
	silence where I walk.

They hear the Siren Song from afar. ADRIAN and ORSINO are transported

ADRIAN	I hear the sound of everything that fears me...
ORSINO	The thing I once called love is not – what *this* is...

They wander in the direction of the Song. CORALINE sees us again

CORALINE	The rainbow reappears, the lords and ladies
	listening to my fresh perceptions. First:
	if my name is Coraline – which I remind you
	it is – that was Orsino in a dress.
	I hate to spoil a story. When I was small,
	there was once some local scandal that my mother
	relished the spreading of, but halfway through
	I cried out 'Maybe the boy was a girl in disguise!'
	I was packed off to bed as if I'd ruined it.
	Ah well, one dolt in black has found his double,
	and befriends him like a fool befriends a mirror.

The Song fades and CORALINE is alone again

CORALINE	As distinct from your lonely fool. She merely thinks
	she's got a hundred followers. *[herself/audience]*

CORALINE runs off after ADRIAN and ORSINO

SCENE VII

The CAPTAIN and MARY come, following the Song as it rises again

CAPTAIN	When our first kiss has ended –
MARY	He will see me –
CAPTAIN	Our second will begin –
MARY	He'll be amazed

I came this far for him –

CAPTAIN   We'll count the hours
we were apart –

MARY   I'll say my lady greets you –

CAPTAIN   And burn them on a bonfire so bright
the stars will blink in wonder –

MARY   And *I* greet you,
I greet you too, sir, Mary, Marianne
Belch I'll say, I'll belch it to thin air,
as a word I'll never waste my breath to mutter –

CAPTAIN   And through the Gate of Moai –

MARY   Through the Gate –

CAPTAIN   Is reconciliation –

MARY   Recognition –

CAPTAIN   Is ecstasy –

MARY   Forgiveness –

CAPTAIN   Oh the world
exactly like the world I knew –

MARY   The world
I knew made new, made good, made right, made true –

CAPTAIN	MARY
When our first kiss has ended	*I'll say I greet you too, sir*
Our second will begin	*I came so far for you*
Through the Gate of Moai	*Through the Gate of Moai*

> The MILLIONAIRE, the LADY and the GENTLEMEN come too, all heading the same
> way, joining the unison

GENTLEMAN	LADY
You're wearing what you wore	*I knew at the steeplechasing*
We walked the Roman walls	*A ring for you my darling*
Beyond the Gate of Moai	*Go through the Gate of Moai*

MILLIONAIRE
The Grand Reunion Ball
For all the world we know
Is through the Gate of Moai

> ALL see a gate ahead of them and move towards it, as suddenly JAGO appears,
> hooded, as if demented, mud caked around his ears

JAGO   In the name of what is holy, don't go there!

I've been there and there's nothing, only rocks
and snakes and precipices! There's no Moai!
There's a madman and a woman and she hates me,
she has the planets watching me, she wants me,
the flies are out to get me, go no further,
dreamers, it's no dream!

Oblivious, the MILLIONAIRE and the lovers dance. JAGO beseeches MARY

JAGO   I'll be revenged on the whole pack of you!

MARY stops and turns

JAGO   I'll be revenged on the whole pack of you!

MARY   Why do you say – those words?

CAPTAIN   Is that the man?
Are you Moai?

MARY   Hush. Why do you say those words?
Mal – *volio*?

CAPTAIN   His ears are stuffed with earth.

JAGO   Follow, follow, follow, hear my story!
Don't go through the gate, follow, follow,
follow, hear my story!

JAGO backs into the trees, beckoning them

MARY   It's not him.

CAPTAIN   Time passed, how would *you* know?

MARY   How would *you* know?

CAPTAIN   He's mad, this place is Moai, *he* is Moai!
My reward for catching him is my heart's desire!
You stay and sing a chorus, he's *mine*.

The CAPTAIN draws his dagger and goes after JAGO. MARY follows him

The MILLIONAIRE and the lovers go dreaming on their way

ADRIAN runs on, with ORSINO his dramatic lady-hostage, and CORALINE his exhausted fool. ADRIAN finds his trusty audience member

ADRIAN   I am told that for the next twenty minutes
nothing will happen here. You may come and go,
no questions asked, a blind eye will be turned.
That's all. Twenty minutes. This never happened.

ADRIAN runs off with ORSINO and CORALINE stumbling behind. The Song fades

ACT THREE

SCENE I

JAGO comes

JAGO   Use no daggers, friends, and look none either.
              The truth's no more than what I can remember.

MALVOLIO, twelve years ago, walks into the empty space, and says to nobody

MALVOLIO   I'll be revenged on the whole pack of you!

He storms off. Then he comes back, with suitcases, raging at thin air

MALVOLIO   Belch, you empty barrel, Toby Belch,
              that pebbles rattle round perpetually
              as you tumble down a drop toward your wreckage,
              I mean you! Yes and you, Sir Aguecheek,
              you elongated shadow cast at evening
              at close of days in which was accomplished nothing,
              you I include! And you, twin-visaged harlot,
              sneering, conniving namesake of Our Lady,
              keeper of the keys that merely *open*,
              never a thought to silence or safekeeping,
              you most of all to blame! And my black-clad mistress,
              mourning creature grinning to the altar,
              somewhere in some far Illyria
              your letter's true and words are true, and *you* are,
              and what I would have you do you do
              and what I would have you be you are
              by and by, what *I* would have you,
              true and you are
              O in some – far –

MALVOLIO begins a journey round in circles, as JAGO comes, stepping in and out of the scene to describe it

JAGO   I first heard him
              some ten, twelve years ago, in a forest clearing.
              A crowd came. The children found him odd

and the adults sad, but he was so – entertaining.
He could really see the people he would rage at.
At first he was encumbered with his baggage,
but he left it in his wake as he meandered
higher up the foothills.

MALVOLIO   I would have you
mourning creature most of all O
do you what you be you what you
only you and by and by you
be you what you

JAGO   As time went by
his curse began to ripen into mishmash,
the words reordered, like a day at night
remembering itself.

MALVOLIO   would you be A
will be I
by and by O
all you would be *will* be only
be it so I
be it so ma
volio ma
volio ma
volio

*Soon MALVOLIO is a stooping old man with a stick, rags for clothes, his only
possession his 'MOAI' letter. MARY and the CAPTAIN are listening to the story*

JAGO   Time swept by like a child
and spun him round for sport. I did that, too. –
Sit down, listen, lady, sir, my name
is Jago, I'm a son of the woods, my tale
condemns its teller, I've done no good on earth
and I want the earth to know it.

CAPTAIN   Son of the woods,
for sure, the earth is running to his ears.

JAGO   Don't fear me, sir, lady, fear the song
this soil protects me from.

CAPTAIN   How will we know
your story's true?

MARY   By listening to it, fool.

CAPTAIN	Fool? I'm a sea-captain!
MARY	Yeah, up a mountain.
JAGO	I lived as a troubadour, I roamed the state
	on scraps and change the rich let fall like litter.
	It was boom-time in the city. Not up here.
	Then one spring the voice stopped,
	like an animal we'd gazed into extinction.
	Reckoned he'd died perhaps, we'd had a vicious
	winter in the mountains.
CAPTAIN	And you never
	thought to find him shelter that whole winter?
MARY	Nothing entertaining in starvation.
JAGO	Neglectful, cold, your worst opinion of me's
	warm compared to mine. But I found him.

MALVOLIO, smiling, sings to himself, sees things

JAGO	His creatures still persisted in the air.
	Mostly I think a lady he could see there
	and always had a care to, clothing her
	in cold or he would fan her the few times
	the sun got glimpses of him. Other days
	his enemies came back and he would dance
	a ring around that zero where his love lay.

MALVOLIO sees them here and there

MARY	I can see the ghosts he saw, I know their names.
JAGO	They were as good as *there*, so when one morning
	a woman came I thought he'd conjured *her*...

SONGBIRD comes out of the trees and observes MALVOLIO

JAGO	It was one of his good days. He made his sounds.
	She sang his sounds, as if to tell the angels
	where she was, that she'd be gone a while
	for she had work to do.
	But she never spoke a word in my hearing.
	She only sang, so I always called her Songbird.
SONGBIRD	*What you would be*
	Will be
	Aye

By and by
All you would be will be
Only you and only
What you would be...

JAGO You see I cram the muck into my ears
just telling you the story.

MARY I can hear her...

CAPTAIN *[to MARY]* She's telling us to come, she's telling us
to leave this misery to his muddy fable.

JAGO You can't, it's just an echo, an imprint,
what you're hearing is my story, so follow...

Folks have come to hear the Song: three WOOD FOLK who would become the
'MILLIONAIRE', the 'GENTLEMAN' and the 'LADY'

JAGO Shyly from the trees they came, wood-folk
who'd never heard a bird sing like Songbird.
And he could see what no one could. He rose
and went among these guileless people, seeing
what he could see around them, here a wedding,
lamp-lit lawns and treasures in great chambers,
marble, satin, waterfalls and wine,
here a house, a palace, a great pool
perfumed with lilac, there on the sloping grasses
assemblies of devoted people gazing...
He hung his smile on them, as Songbird sang.
Made stars of them, and statues, and stones.

The WOOD-FOLK see their dreams coming true

JAGO They wandered home to huts and woodland holes
they could no longer see.

MARY What about you?
Did it change you?

JAGO It did.
I lost my mind. I thought I could see before me
a woman who could love me. From that day
I was Songbird's to command.

JAGO joins in the song. SONGBIRD sees him and dances with him. They whirl
MALVOLIO round like a toy, cruelly, but on he dances, beaming

MALVOLIO	SONGBIRD
By and by and be it so	*What you would be*
Ma lolio ma lolio	*Will be*
JAGO	*Aye*
Everything that's coming came	*By and by*
Tomorrow and today	*What you would be will be*
GENTLEMAN/LADY	*Only you and only*
This is the only moment	*What you would be*
That we meet and so is this one,O	*Will be*
MILLIONAIRE	*Aye*
Everyone who walked away	*By and by*
Has never walked away	*What you would be will be*

When the Song ends, SONGBIRD, MALVOLIO and the WOOD-FOLK are gone. But we can hear the Song still, far-off, outside JAGO's story. JAGO freezes

JAGO   That's her. She knows I'm here. Follow, follow!
That star is staring at me, it's the dog-star,
she keeps it as a dog, it winks at her
so follow, follow please, hear my story!

JAGO runs into the trees. MARY follows, the CAPTAIN stops her

CAPTAIN   You can't believe this fellow.

MARY   I could see him.

CAPTAIN   Who?

MARY   Moai, Malvolio, in my mind.
He was written a letter once
that showed him a sweet garden
there never was. He's dwelt there ever since.
We broke him. I can save him. And this wretch
will take me where he is.

CAPTAIN   The song is *that* way.
Higher up the mountain – our mission!
Your Moai, my Paloma. Where the song is,
the Gate is, and they are. The other way!
What I would be will be... O Paloma,
it's this way – Mary Belch?

MARY has run off after JAGO. The CAPTAIN runs after her

SCENE II

The Song rises as ADRIAN *comes, then* CORALINE, *holding* ORSINO *prisoner. They are all under the song's influence*

ADRIAN   'What I would be will be', did you hear the words?
Then it goes 'Adrian', yes, 'by and by, Adrian'
somehow it scans, 'your dream will come true, by and by,
Adrian' – that's the refrain – and it reminds me
of *the exact same words* my mother
never said to me, *the exact same words,*
to the letter, 'by and by, sweet Adrian,
your dreams will come true'. They did do, regardless,
actually. For, now I have a hostage,
nothing can stop my arrow.

CORALINE   It comes again,
the rainbow of lords and ladies, always wondering
how will Coraline put this right? I see you,   *[audience]*
I owe you, I know you, we are friends.

ORSINO   I do this for Cesario, poor fool
who little knows he leads his old master.
His dark new master is my dark new foe.
As *Man* I know he is the whip-sharp agent
of my policy, but as *Woman* I know nothing.
He is my foe. Cesario is his fool.
Oh, nothing more to him nor me. My will
is my Assassin's will, I need no eyes
to see but his. Blindly I follow Blindman!

They move on into the trees, the Song fading

SCENE III

SONGBIRD *comes with* MALVOLIO. MARY *and the* CAPTAIN *listening*

MARY   If she could sing so well, why did you need *him*?

JAGO   Because he could truly see what he could see.
I tried it but the folks would melt away,
scoff at it, see through it. Him they believed.

CAPTAIN   Your 'Songbird' never spoke?

JAGO   She only sang.
                 When he was sleeping (when he wouldn't sleep   *[Malvolio]*
                 we made him sleep, she knew her roots and plants)
                 we slept together. *What I would be, was.*

MARY   That was *your* dream, what was hers?
                 What was the song to her?

JAGO   The song is power.
                 It drew you here, it draws you like it drew
                 the woodland-people and the city-folk.
                 The villages are dead, the river's dammed
                 with all the dumped possessions of those dreamers.
                 The mountain's hers.

CAPTAIN   What does she want it for?

JAGO   I don't know what she wants.
                 They say you can see the whole world from the summit.
                 Maybe she wants that next.

CAPTAIN   So you needed Moai
                 for your circus act. What did *he* get from this?

JAGO   He had no other life. We had a rope.

MARY   Mercy me.

JAGO   He shared in what we had.

CAPTAIN   What did you have?

JAGO   Have? We had the lot.
                 Tens, hundreds, thousands, over the horizon.
                 Every man or woman we encountered,
                 we'd ask them would you like to know your fortune?
                 Dumb they'd stand there fumbling in their pockets,
                 they couldn't understand what wasn't there,
                 but then *he* began to speak, demented Moai,
                 and she to sing, my unrelenting Songbird,
                 till every thought had turned into a wish
                 and every wish had twisted to desire.

The WOOD-FOLK keep seeing new wonders, switching instantly

JAGO   A lovesick fool would hear of adoration –
                 a lonely soul of company forever –
                 the poor man of a golden throne – the luckless
                 of dice with sixes on all seven faces –
                 the fat made fine – the dismal made divine –

disfigured men perfected in the mirrors
hanging in thin air – old ladies dancing
in the first years of the last century...

MARY   And you sold them this.

JAGO   Yes. Not at first, but yes.
The joy we gave them, lady, we three!

MARY   The joy they gave you, chum, obviously.

JAGO   I hadn't looked for it. It was, it was Moai,
and Songbird.

MARY   And you were what, the merchant.

JAGO   Do I look prosperous to you?

MARY   They do say
stocks can fall as well as rise.

JAGO   Our stock
went skyward, moonward, starward.
For the more we asked of people,
one kroner, two, five, ten, a golden schilling,
ten, fifty, hundreds, thousands,
the more we asked the more they came to find us,
like the price itself, the *word* for price, had swollen
to paradise. So the rumours spread downriver
and then came everyone.

CAPTAIN   So what's the Gate?

JAGO   The whole wood was our market, hundreds now
were pining for the prophecies of Moai.
We needed a pinnacle, a destination,
a promise beyond promises. So we built
the Gate, and we said that – everyone you loved,
had ever loved, living or dead, was through it.

CAPTAIN   And are they?

MARY   Are you out of your mind? Of course not.

CAPTAIN   I – sorry – it was – the story.

MARY   So what happened?
Why are your singing angel and her creature
living it up with your untold stolen money
while you go hungry here?

JAGO   It's hard to say.

MARY   You've said you shook a thousand people down

for all they had and sold them thin air,
how hard can it be?

JAGO   I'll show how hard
by telling it. I'll tell you why I left her.
An old man came our way, some solitary
who'd once imagined gardens of granddaughters,
but love had passed him by.

An OLD MAN comes, gives away his last possession

SONGBIRD   *What you would be*
Will be
Aye
By and by
All you would be will be
Only you and only
What you would be...

JAGO   And that poor withered stump heard lullabies
he sang to his cradling arms. Then he was gone,
transported, empty-handed but transported
all the same. But he wasn't the only one
the melody had touched.

MIRALDA appears, holding a shawl she thinks is a baby

JAGO   A child had walked,
young, comfortless and cold and miles from home.
Now her shawl was a child to her and her mind was gone.
She wandered up to us.
I'd seen her eyes before, those yearning eyes,
but neither woman showed the faintest sign
one even knew the other.
When Songbird sang, a mother sang to her baby.
When Songbird stopped, a child stood with nothing.
Songbird made it clear we had no time
for those who couldn't pay, we were travelling on.

SONGBIRD leads MALVOLIO away by the rope

JAGO   And I meant to cry to Songbird – this child
knows you, she's walked the world to find you!
For I saw her eyes flash once and then go out.
I knew she knew her daughter. But she went,

and I went too, leaving the child alone,
none of my business.

CAPTAIN   We know all about your business.

MIRALDA wanders back into the woods. JAGO is alone with his story

MARY   So you ran away?

JAGO   She's close, she knows I'm here –
the time between her songs is known to me
like the time between my heartbeats and it's getting
short –

MARY   You made your stand.

JAGO   That young girl's eyes
were in my mind at waking –
and I thought of all the money we'd taken,
and the standing corpses of our customers
I daily glimpsed, all festering in silence,
waiting to hear their song. Without the song
their lives to them are nothing. You don't *know* her!
Whoever passes through the Gate of Moai
is as much her slave as that poor lunatic
who planted the whole seed of this deception!
They'll die if she wants and if she wants they'll kill us!

MARY   Malvolio is there, or what was once
Malvolio...

CAPTAIN   And my Paloma too...
Paloma's childhood dreams
were of great fame, world fame, I see her now
performing in her rags, in her delusion...

MARY   Poor steward of the house...

JAGO   We can't go there!
We are three, she has an army!

CAPTAIN   Listen, mud-man,
I come with this Sealed Order from the Duke,
I have his authority to return that lost
soul of a steward home to Illyria,
and, if I do, the Duke will find my love,
for I know my lady's here, look here's the Duke *[sealed order]*
in black and whi – and – here's the Duke in black...

The CAPTAIN has just read the Sealed Order. MARY takes it from him

MARY   'Dear The Blindman, when you have found this Moai,
eliminate him; and the boatman too;
also despatch the woman. Leave no trace
this mission ever was. Finally: eat this.'
You – haven't obeyed the order.

CAPTAIN   I'm – not hungry.

MARY   You yourself would *be* the only trace,
Blindman, so, how'd you rate your chances
with Orsino down below?

CAPTAIN   It's – worse than that.
They're going to send The Blindman.

MARY   *You're* The Blindman.
You're – not The Blindman. Lovely. What was that then,
another campfire story?

CAPTAIN   It was Otto,
he said I'd find my love upriver – I just
clambered aboard.

MARY   Oh yes, I can see how that's
completely Otto's fault.

CAPTAIN   In a way.

MARY   Oh God.
So you were going to kill us all, Blindman.
Only, you're *not* The Blindman, are you. Only,
someone is. And he's probably watching us,
and if we go through the Gate and we find Moai
and the snakes don't bite, *he will,* and he'll kill the man
I came to save. I'll have saved Malvolio
like a dog a bone, for later. If we stay here
Blindman will pick us off, and if we turn back
we'll meet him on the trail. We're dead three ways,
so someone light a fire, let's toast our luck
on skewers.

CAPTAIN   What I did I did for love.

MARY   Some misremembered hazy yellow summer
flaps in your dry brain like a canary.
No. What you did you did for a fading picture
hanging round your neck, and now
it hangs round mine as well, and it's getting tighter.
Let's die with my old master. This direction.

MARY and the CAPTAIN run on towards the Gate

JAGO	There I won't go. I couldn't stop them going.
	I was the cause, I'll flee with the effects.

JAGO flees the other way, but straight into ADRIAN, followed by CORALINE with ORSINO hostage. ADRIAN has his dagger to JAGO's throat

ADRIAN	Threaten my hostage, would you?	
JAGO	Sorry – what?	
ADRIAN	You are talking to The Blindman.	
JAGO	I am?	
ADRIAN	Clearly you know the name.	
JAGO	Actually no.	
ADRIAN	Fool, make our threat.	
CORALINE	Our threat. What's our threat?	
ADRIAN	Tell us the whereabouts of the Impostor,	
	the Woman, and the Boatman, or this Lady	*[Orsino]*
	dies.	
JAGO	I'm sorry, I haven't met the lady.	
CORALINE	Boss, it helps if the lady's something *to* him,	
	I mean, in hostage work.	
ADRIAN	So, introduce them.	
CORALINE	Stranger, hostage, hostage, stranger.	
ADRIAN	Good.	
ORSINO	Don't kill me, please!	
JAGO	Don't kill her.	
ADRIAN	See, it worked.	
	Watch, and learn. – Fool, inform the hostage	
	we don't *mean* we will kill her. She's our hostage	
	and vital to our plan.	
CORALINE	Boss, that's, good,	
	humane, in many ways, but it's even better	
	if you don't let this man *hear* that you don't mean	*[Jago]*
	you're really going to kill her.	
ADRIAN *[to JAGO]*	Is he right?	
JAGO	Well yes, it makes a difference.	
ADRIAN	Hm. Clever.	
	So...how do we use the hostage?	

ORSINO   I'm all right
                to sit this one out, you know, lord.

ADRIAN   Be silent!
                You'll not be harmed, for now.

JAGO   I've no idea
                what woman, or what boatman or impostor
                you're on about.

ADRIAN   Why is there mud in your ears...

JAGO   Why? I've been a hostage.

ADRIAN   I see.

[to CORALINE] Put mud in her ears.

ORSINO   No, save me, I will swoon!

ORSINO swoons, CORALINE catches him

CORALINE   Oh for heaven's sake.

JAGO   Please don't put mud in her ears.

ADRIAN   We have him now! He's putty in our hands!
                Tell us the whereabouts of the fugitives
                noted above and we shall spare the hostage
                besplatterment of the ears.

JAGO   I don't know them!

ADRIAN   Still he holds out, the monster! D'you not care
                if the lady's ears are smeared i'the mire?

JAGO   Do you really
                want me to answer that?

ADRIAN   Um. *[to CORALINE]* Do I?

CORALINE   Boss, I think we have a Bohemian stand-off.
                None of us can remember what we wanted.
                Perhaps you should lower your weapon.

ADRIAN   Know this, fool:
                I will fight to the death to protect this precious hostage.
                She is vital.

CORALINE   I'm not sure that the word *hostage*
                means quite what you think it does.

ADRIAN   No time
                for your wordplay, fool, it – doesn't matter...

The Song comes again, close by, all around them, affecting them

ADRIAN We need no information. I will find them...
And any man who seeks to harm my hostage
will know as he dies that he just met The Blindman...

ORSINO *[to CORALINE]* Bear me, honest fool, my constitution
is delicate. At these high altitudes
to swoon is second nature...

CORALINE Oh I've got you,
hostage-lady, and I've got this feeling
your chance of escaping life as The Blindman's hostage
is the same as your chance of escaping life as a lady...

ORSINO Was that to me?

CORALINE No, friend, to the rainbow. *[the audience]*

The three hurry away towards the music, JAGO flees the other way

SCENE IV

The song is now pure music. MARY and the CAPTAIN come, enthralled

CAPTAIN I see the Gate –

MARY Remember why we came here –

CAPTAIN For love, we came for love –

MARY I don't think so,
but I can't remember why, if it wasn't love,
I have a letter, here, it will put all wrongs
to right –

CAPTAIN I have a picture of my future,
though I plucked it from the past, there is no past,
it's all that's left –

*Into the music come a different woman's voice and a guitar, and light coming
from the Gate. MARY and the CAPTAIN kneel*

CAPTAIN You hear her, she's there,
Paloma, I found you, hear me! It's – it's –
what's my name?

MARY I come for Malvolio,
I'm here to take him home!

The guitar is OTTO's, and the voice MIRALDA's. They appear

SONG   *What you would be*
                May be
                Aye
                May not, may be
                Tread carefully
                Go tree by tree
                Go watchfully
                Aye
                Hurt not me
                And I'll walk with thee

   The CAPTAIN sees MIRALDA as his Paloma, and is transfixed

CAPTAIN   Those – are not the words.

OTTO   They are this evening,
           boss, for one night only.

CAPTAIN   How – are *you* there?

OTTO   I'm a ferryman, remember,
           I walk through doors and gates both ways, you should try it.

MARY   Where – is the music?

OTTO   Where? You can hear the music.

MARY   I hear birdsong.

OTTO   There's nothing *but* birdsong.

CAPTAIN   Paloma!

OTTO   Boss, you look as if your compass
           claims your island's here but you're on the ocean.

CAPTAIN   The past – *present* –

OTTO   Let me present the past,
           my pioneers, or at least the last few moments.
           My heartbeat here goes by the name Miralda.
           Miralda met her mother.

MIRALDA   All I wanted
           were her eyes to look in mine.

OTTO   But she went on singing.

MIRALDA   Or her voice to say my name.

OTTO   But she went on singing.

MIRALDA   Or her arms for once to hold me.

OTTO   But she turned
           and sang, her back to us.

MIRALDA	She shut her eyes
	and sang as if to sing the light away.
OTTO	But the light held still. She shot a glance at us.
MIRALDA	Her eyes so wild to see us unafraid.
OTTO	Her eyes so hot she must have thought by now
	we'd melt away but then, she's not met Otto,
	and I sang Miralda *my* songs.
MIRALDA	*We Stand Here!*
OTTO	*We Breathe!*
MIRALDA	*And Still We Grow!*
OTTO	*The Ground Is Rough!*
MIRALDA	*Your Hand In Mine!*
OTTO	*Our Life Begun!*
MIRALDA	*The Earth*
	Enough For Us!
OTTO	Her voice began to weaken.
MIRALDA	And her eyes were white until they shut.
OTTO	Her song
	was fierce until it faded to the breeze.
MIRALDA	Where a blackbird took it up like he'd just found it.
OTTO	And a sparrow like he said *I found it first,*
	then a magpie said *In fact I wrote this song.*
MIRALDA	So it spread through the tall heavens of the forest.
OTTO	And we don't know where she went. There's a rising track
	that snakes about the summit and beyond
	to the further mountains. We saw twigs and pebbles
	scuffle down that track and lie still.
MIRALDA	And then we saw the people.
OTTO	Hollow faces
	staring from the open mouths of caves,
	waiting, as if for nothing.
MIRALDA	Hundreds of them.
	And what did you sing?
OTTO	A song about how seeds
	and blueberries grow here and you had better
	eat them or you'll die.
MIRALDA	That was not the title!

OTTO	That was the gist. Captain, Blindman, boss,
	you look the same as they do.
CAPTAIN	I – I do not
	understand –
OTTO	My heartbeat's from where *you* are.
MIRALDA	I'm from Carinthia, sir, and I came here
	some time ago, my illness won't say when.
	I grew up in a valley hedged about
	with dense woods. My Otto thinks you know it.
CAPTAIN	Know it, I – I left it last summer,
	to follow you – your name is not Miralda –
OTTO	Her name is Miralda, boss, her compass works.
MIRALDA	I left my home, because, for the third time,
	my mother went away. My two great-aunts
	were kind, they said she always goes away
	because she has a *destiny*, except –
	it was always a different destiny – a poet,
	a painter, or a dancer, or a healer –
	I noticed as I grew up, all that ever
	stayed the same was: *I* stayed in the valley,
	she stayed far away. They said she'd always
	been that way, ever since she was sixteen
	and ran away to change the world one summer.
CAPTAIN	One summer...
MIRALDA	That was twenty years ago,
	the first time. The last time I came looking,
	I stowed away to Illyria, met some folks
	who told me everything I ever wanted
	was to be found upriver. So I walked,
	I scrambled and I clambered and I climbed,
	and one warm day at noon I thought I heard her,
	she sang to me and I ran so fast towards her –
	it was in a clearing where the light was amber...
	beyond that I don't think I can remember,
	or nothing till I heard this minstrel singing *[Otto]*
	a verse about a squirrel falling down!
	Which, when my eyes came open, I could see,
	and I found myself wrapped up on a little tree-stump,
	one of two people laughing at life together.

The CAPTAIN, *dazed, wanders off and sits down alone*

MARY	Captain. Captain –
CAPTAIN	Turn your boat around.
	This isle is uninhabited.
OTTO	Miralda...

OTTO *signals for* MIRALDA *to go, and she exits*

OTTO *[to MARY]* I'm sorry I, feel I, left you in the lurch there,
back there along the trail. You had each other.

MARY Each other? He's in love with his own necklace.   *[Captain]*
And the man *I* came for's probably in his grave.

OTTO He's no March hare but he's quicker than a dead man.

MIRALDA *gently leads* MALVOLIO *into view. He is far gone now*

MARY Not even the smile is left...

MIRALDA We found the poor soul
tied to a rock.

OTTO *[to MARY]*   Will you not show your face?

MARY Not to that man or any. There's a house
I set a match to long ago.

MARY, *like the* CAPTAIN, *wanders off and sits down alone*

MIRALDA He eats the berries, love, he knows to eat them.

OTTO So while that's true, it's what we'll settle for.

Suddenly ADRIAN *leaps in, dagger drawn, holding it to the throat of* MALVOLIO.
MIRALDA *and* OTTO *back away in terror*

ADRIAN Prepare to perish, Moai, I have found you!
I say *prepare* but there's little preparation
involved at your end. Die now like the dog
you may well be, it's not as if I know you,
but I know you have committed manifold
crimes against the Capital, and it's only
my instinctive silence stopping me from naming
one by one your many, many treasons!

OTTO He's done no wrong!

MIRALDA He's old, he's lost his mind!

ADRIAN Stand back, accomplices, I have a hostage
and, if you harm her, I shall have no choice

but to do what I did to the warlike Red Rodolfo!
Or possibly what I did to the Archduke Franz
Fitz Frederick, though I don't have the equipment.

CORALINE comes, dragging ORSINO

CORALINE	Blindman, boss, you don't know who this is!	*[Orsino]*
ORSINO	*I* don't know who I am!	
CORALINE	Your name's Olivia.	

There was a story, ten, twelve years ago
in Illyria, this was, my mother told me,
I've been thinking about the details, how perhaps
untangling that untangles this – this lady
was loved by the Duke Orsino, the great man
who sent you here. This poor old wretch you threaten
was her steward, he was dear to her. Orsino
would never harm a soul Olivia
cared for. Say, my lady, is it not so?

ORSINO   Well...

CORALINE   And I, though in this company
I count for naught, if anyone should prize me,
know that I prize peacefulness, and mercy,
and the healing force of time, above all things.

ORSINO   Well...

CORALINE   So factor that in your thoughts. Lady.

ORSINO   Olivia, yes, that's me. I am a hostage,
obviously, as you see, I'm this man's hostage,
but in daily life I am – Olivia,
the lady, Lady Olivia, that's me,
and Orsino, that great man, did love me once,
and I was a fool to let him go. Oh, curses!
He was such a cool, strong man, Orsino. Well,
ancient history yes, but you, my captor,   *[Adrian]*
my bandit, my assassin, my dark gaoler,
I would have you let this man alone, for old times.

ADRIAN sheathes his dagger

ADRIAN   My hostage speaks. Nobody even *think*
of harming her. Stand back! Ancient fellow,
you are free to live. For now.

ADRIAN returns to ORSINO's side. MIRALDA comforts MALVOLIO

MARY draws out her crumpled letter and approaches ORSINO (Olivia)

MARY	My lady, you know all about the face
	you're looking at.
ORSINO	I do?
CORALINE	(Mary Belch,
	used to be your housemaid.)
ORSINO	Ah, Mary.
	Yes. Carry on.
MARY	This man you see, your steward,
	exploited and abandoned, he lies nowhere
	but at my door. This letter,
	I should read it aloud to him. My voice, today,
	has not the spine for it, will you please read it?
CORALINE	(Yes. I will.)
ORSINO	I will.
CORALINE	(Right now.)
ORSINO	Right now.

MARY gives him the letter. ORSINO addresses MALVOLIO

ORSINO	Ahem. Handwriting's awful.
CORALINE	That's right,
	you always wrote so carelessly, did you not?
ORSINO	Er yes, indeed. 'My dear – Manvolio,
	you have been most wronged and most notoriously
	have been...a bus.' What's a bus?
CORALINE	Abused, my lady.
ORSINO	Of course, it's so long ago, '...have been abused,
	and I hold myself to blame for the event.
	My mind was turned...by lice.'
CORALINE	Let's have a look...
ORSINO	It was turned by lice.
CORALINE	It's not i.c., it's o.v.,
	my lady, again.
ORSINO/	'My mind was turned by love – '
OLIVIA	/My mind was turned by love...

OLIVIA appears out of nowhere, knowing the letter by heart, takes the letter from ORSINO, kneels down by MALVOLIO

OLIVIA	...and I had no care
	for a gentleman who for so many years
	had nothing on his mind but care for me.
	I wish that gentleman to know that one day,
	be it today, tomorrow, or his last,
	my last or the world's, his honourable position
	at the head of my poor house will wait for him
	perpetually, yours ever: Olivia.

MALVOLIO doesn't stir, no one stirs. OLIVIA rises, leaving the letter in MALVOLIO's hands

OLIVIA	Too late a deliverance.
MARY	My – my lady!
OLIVIA	Maria.
MARY	Oh my lady.
OLIVIA	Have I found
	Illyria? It isn't where I left it.
	I woke this morning in my hilltop house,
	from a dream in which my husband sails his lightship
	over the olive groves and not the ocean.
	And I thought the world so quiet I peered out
	through veiling curtains at the sunny prospect,
	the town spread out below, the port, the sea.
	Well sure I must be dreaming still, I murmured,
	for I saw *myself,* far off, in my mourning-clothes,
	trotting along the streets. At once I dressed,
	I walked, I ran, I shadowed her, I lost her.
	Illyria was deserted. Where had I gone?
	I was giddy with having gone – where had the *world* gone?
	At the palace of the Duke there was no Duke
	nor man nor woman either – only music,
	only the wind, a ghost about the stairwells,
	corridors and chambers, only the wind
	that breathed the pipes and horns, caressed the strings,
	tickled the skins of drums. The Duke has vanished:
	music plays, a thoroughly modern music.
	And here's myself at last. How do you do, *[Orsino]*
	sweet fugitive?

ADRIAN   Lady, upon what cause
                     do you thus impersonate my precious hostage,
                     the Lady Olivia?

OLIVIA *[to ORSINO]* The Lady Olivia, *me*,
                     can you answer this fierce fellow?

ORSINO   I'm – his hostage.
                     I am – constrained.

OLIVIA   Is it *you* – my dear *Rossina!*

ORSINO   I'm who, sorry?

OLIVIA   Rossina, my dear cuz!
                     I've not set eyes on you since we were tomboys,
                     and then your family moved into the mountains,
                     didn't you?

ORSINO   Um –

CORALINE   (We did.)

ORSINO   We did indeed.

OLIVIA   How dear Rossina loved to play the game
           of you-be-me-and-I'll-be-you, remember?
           You were close to Orsino, weren't you, in the old days?

ORSINO   Somewhat, yes.

OLIVIA   Which is why it's so delightful
           that now he's disappeared I've once again
           found my Rossina, my dearest cuz.

CORALINE *[to ORSINO]*   That *is*
                     delightful, isn't it, lady?

ORSINO   Very much so.

OLIVIA   I wonder if we'll ever *see* Orsino
           hereafter, I always thought he had this look
           that seemed to say there were new worlds to explore
           beyond his muddy dukedom. Did you think so,
           Rossina, did you think the same about him.

ORSINO   I did, oh yes. I too
           do not expect we will see that man again,
           that sensitive man, farewell.

CORALINE   Lady Olivia –

ORSINO   Yes?

OLIVIA   Yes?

ORSINO   Oh, sorry. Force of habit.

CORALINE	How have you come? The river's perilous.
OLIVIA	Not to a freshly-minted mariner.

CORALINE   How have you come? The river's perilous.

OLIVIA   Not to a freshly-minted mariner.
            I had to get *something* out of my oceanic
            husband, so I got him to teach me sailing,
            which, having done, once more he sailed away.

CORALINE   Is that why you wear black?

OLIVIA   You're not familiar
            with many women my age, are you, darling.

ADRIAN comes forward

ADRIAN   Lady Olivia, the inexplicable absence
            of the Duke who hired me for my secret mission
            relieves me of that mission. I am The Blindman,
            a silent man of whom you know nothing,
            of my childhood, education (education?
            ha!) for I keep silent on such matters,
            but moments come in life that call for action
            and, in extremity, I do speak forth.
            – Lady Rossina, though I release you gladly
            from your duties as a hostage, I invite you
            instead to become, in secret, known to no man,
            The Blindman's Lady. Send me on my missions,
            allow me special license, reward me,
            know only what I know.

OLIVIA   Why, Rossina,
            take them while they're hot, we used to cry
            when they brought the cakes out, take them while they're
                                              piping!

ORSINO   I am all hostage, sir. Let us explore.

ADRIAN and ORSINO embrace, and exit

OLIVIA   Malvolio? Can you see the world go round?

MIRALDA   I think it goes round him, my lady, but see
            his eyes see something.

MARY   Pray they don't see me.

OLIVIA   Maria, we'll take him home with us.

MARY   My lady,
            twelve years your home has not been home for me.
            I married your uncle Toby.

OLIVIA	So you did.
MARY	The Duke was to release me from that bond but the Duke has gone and my name is Mary Belch.
OLIVIA	Your name is Mary Belch but the bond is gone, Maria. Sheets of paper in the palace blew across a room to me in armfuls: one told me Toby died a month ago, alone in the empty house of a stranger's daughter, bellowing for someone, *anyone* to row him up the river into Moai.
MARY *[to herself]*	So fare thee well, old sack. I said I'd beat you.
OLIVIA	You are the Widow Mary now, we two will close our books and scan the blue horizon.

MARY kneels beside MALVOLIO, who is staring vacantly at the letter

MARY	Malvolio, we have our places back. If you promise to be as irritable as ever I will irritate you by the day, the hour, the moment, what you will. – Well. Still nothing. We may take him, if only into care.
MALVOLIO	I – ivory –
MARY	What?
MALVOLIO	I – *ivory* –
OLIVIA	He reads my letter upside down. Malvolio, are you there?
MARY	There's something else, it's my old writing –
MALVOLIO	It's – it's – it's – *ivory for special!* Always, always, look, she's written, stupid woman, wooden forks and spoons, not on a *Sunday*, it's ivory for special! Are you foolish?

MALVOLIO rises, thrusting the letter back to MARY

MALVOLIO	Are we running a hovel here or a fine house? Maria, what does this mean?
MARY	Oh glory be the man's himself –
MALVOLIO	I feel I am – not dressed – correctly quite, still, still, that can wait, I shall be satisfied!

MARY	Oh master waiter,
	all manner of things can wait.
MALVOLIO	Wait? Are you mad?
	My lady has guests, look about you, dolt!
MARY	Don't call me –
	patience, patience, look, Malvolio,
	you're waking from your sleep.
MALVOLIO	Then it's six o'clock
	and you ought to be making breakfast! Some are born
	to make breakfast, some are born to serve it,
	and some are born to have it served upon 'em!
MARY	Do I have allies here?
OTTO	It's like you told me,
	lady, this is the man you came to see!
MARY	Well I've seen him now and he's put grey hairs on me
	like he always did.
MALVOLIO	Maria, explain to me
	why you are out of uniform?
MARY	You *what?*
MALVOLIO	My lady shall hear of this!
MARY	Malvolio,
	I have come some way to say – Go shake your ears!

MARY storms away to sit alone

OLIVIA	Malvolio,
	rest, rest, there are no chores to do
	today, we have a journey downriver,
	and then we'll sit and talk about your duties.
	The plates are where you placed them on the day
	you slammed the garden gate. Young gentleman, *[Coraline]*
	help him down the path to where my boat is,
	and you can serve me.
CORALINE	First day, new position!
OLIVIA	Do I know you from somewhere, darling, what's your
	name?
CORALINE	Well my *real* name is Cora – Cesario.
OLIVIA	Really? What a coincidence. Heigh-ho.
	Ferryman, will you follow?

OTTO	Ma'am, there's hundreds
	to be fed, and ferried down from their delusions.
MIRALDA	We'll stay until the mountain's just a mountain.
OLIVIA	Then I thank you both. We will have Illyria back.
	I had better take care of it. – Maria, will you come?
MARY	My lady, reckon I'll find my own way home.

MARY stays sitting alone, as does the CAPTAIN. OLIVIA leaves, with CORALINE leading MALVOLIO. OTTO notices JAGO by a tree

OTTO	I'm a man of to's and fro's, but surely, friend,
	you can see it's all *fro* now, and not a *to*
	in sight.
JAGO	I – want to help. With all those people.
	The wood-folk, in the caves. I think I know
	where every one of them comes from.
OTTO	Then you're welcome,
	for I've not the foggiest clue. You can ferry me!
	He can ferry us, eh Miralda? Altogether:
	Loose the arrow and bowl the ball
	A dream come true's no dream at all

OTTO and MIRALDA make to leave, with JAGO behind. The CAPTAIN rises and stops MIRALDA as she's leaving, offering her the pendant

CAPTAIN	I knew your mother, love.

MIRALDA stops, stares at him, and leaves. The CAPTAIN looks at the pendant. Only he and MARY are left

CAPTAIN	Well. As you say. A captain up a mountain.
MARY	And a housemaid in a jungle.
CAPTAIN	Aren't we two
	the King and Queen of Carnival.
MARY	Just call us
	jokers Red and Black and play your hands
	without us.
CAPTAIN	As you say.
MARY	How could you think
	what happened to you twenty years ago
	happened to you last summer?
CAPTAIN	I – because –
	the years I spent – were always the same year.

Summer, the woods, where is she, every autumn
in cities, every Christmas in a wasteland,
put out to sea in spring. Somehow it felt
like the one and only year.

MARY   You were right the first time:
blind in name and nature.

CAPTAIN   Wait one second,
one-time Lady Belch. At least I didn't
sit twelve years in a kitchen in the service
of pity – oh, not pity for the man
you played upon, but pity for yourself!
At least I saw the world!

MARY   Saw the world?
You saw a pencil sketch
when you could have been seeing life itself. This face
is the first sight you've seen in twenty years!
I mean this *place*. Not face. I mean this clearing.

CAPTAIN   Dead right, and so let's go.

MARY   What?

CAPTAIN   Let's leave it.
Let's never be where we were. Let's only be
where we've just arrived.

MARY   Never – be where we were?

CAPTAIN   Or who we were...

MARY   Or how we were...

CAPTAIN   Let's go then,
Mary – what's your maiden name?

MARY   As you say,
Admiral. Let's never be who we were.

*MARY and the CAPTAIN link arms, and head off into the trees. MARY rips
up the letter from Olivia to Malvolio, and the CAPTAIN tosses the pendant
away*

OTTO playing guitar. The players return as indicated

OTTO & MIRALDA   *Hurt not me and I'll walk with thee*
Though the moon stand still and the time run free
And the path be stone, and the earth alone
And the breath soon done, and the end begun, oh

ALL   *Hurt not me and I'll walk with thee*

JAGO, SONGBIRD,   *Dream, dream, the Illyrian Dream*
& THE WOOD-FOLK   *We are waking up by a sparkling stream*
                             O fool, my fool, the water's cool
                             For the dream was dear but the morning's here, oh
ALL   *Hurt not me and I'll walk with thee*

ADRIAN & ORSINO   *You are mine for now, I am yours for now*
                             But now is forever, don't ask me how
                             We never shall tell though we know damn well
                             Music, play on! Our mission is done, oh
ALL   *Hurt not me and I'll walk with thee*

OLIVIA, CORALINE   *We are ages old, and our tale was told*
& MALVOLIO   *And the lines were learned and the seats were sold*
                             Pardon our play, it's our holiday,
                             Now it's westward-ho to the world we know, oh
ALL   *Hurt not me and I'll walk with thee*

MARY & CAPTAIN   *Remember that day? – No neither do I*
                             There was love in the air – If you say so dear
                             That winter we met – It was autumn we met
                             It was summer, let's say – It'll do for this play, oh
ALL   *Hurt not me and I'll walk with thee*
                             Though the moon stand still and the time run free
                             Though the moon stand still and the time run free
                             Though the moon stand still!

Stop. Bow. And depart

Other titles by Glyn Maxwell include:

Glyn Maxwell: Plays One
9781840025903

Glyn Maxwell: Plays Two
9781840026153

After Troy
9781849430265

Liberty!
9781840028690

The Lion's Face
9781840029949

The Forever Waltz
9781840025910

Mimi and the Stalker
9781840028843

Seven Angels
9781849430791

Merlin and the Woods of Time
9781849432245

On Poetry
9781849430852

WWW.OBERONBOOKS.COM

www.ingramcontent.com/pod-product-compliance
Ingram Content Group UK Ltd.
Pitfield, Milton Keynes, MK11 3LW, UK
UKHW020727280225
455688UK00012B/545